How To Use This Study Guide

This five-lesson study guide corresponds to *"Jesus Is Your Healer" With Denise Renner* (Renner TV). Each lesson in this study guide covers a topic that is addressed during the program series, with questions and references supplied to draw you deeper into your own private study of the Scriptures on this subject.

To derive the most benefit from this study guide, consider the following:

First, watch or listen to the program prior to working through the corresponding lesson in this guide. (Programs can also be viewed at **renner.org** by clicking on the Media/Archives links or on our Renner Ministries YouTube channel.)

Second, take the time to look up the scriptures included in each lesson. Prayerfully consider their application to your own life.

Third, use a journal or notebook to make note of your answers to each lesson's Study Questions and Practical Application challenges.

Fourth, invest specific time in prayer and in the Word of God to consult with the Holy Spirit. Write down the scriptures or insights He reveals to you.

Finally, take action! Whatever the Lord tells you to do according to His Word, do it.

For added insights on this subject, it is recommended that you obtain Denise Renner's book *Jesus Is Your Healer*. You may also select from Rick's and Denise's other available resources by placing your order at **renner.org** or by calling 1-800-742-5593.

TOPIC

Pulling Back the Curtain on Healing

SCRIPTURES

1. **Psalm 103:1-3** (*KJV*) — Bless the Lord, O my soul: and all that is within me, bless his holy name. Bless the Lord, O my soul, and forget not all his benefits: Who forgiveth all thine iniquities; who healeth all thy diseases.

2. **Isaiah 53:4** — Surely He has borne our griefs and carried our sorrows....

3. **Luke 4:18,19** — "The Spirit of the Lord is upon Me, because He has anointed Me to preach the gospel to the poor; He has sent Me to heal the brokenhearted, to proclaim liberty to the captives and recovery of sight to the blind, to set at liberty those who are oppressed; to proclaim the acceptable year of the Lord."

4. **Mark 16:18** — "...They will lay hands on the sick, and they will recover."

5. **1 Peter 2:24** — Who Himself bore our sins in His own body on the tree, that we, having died to sins, might live for righteousness — by whose stripes you were healed.

SYNOPSIS

The five lessons in this study, *Jesus Is Your Healer*, will focus on the following topics:

- Pulling Back the Curtain on Healing
- Faith Stands Still
- Faith That Overcomes the Impossible
- Jesus Is Both Savior and Healer
- Hope Opens the Door for Healing

A Note From Rick Renner

I am on a personal quest to see a "revival of the Bible" so people can establish their lives on a firm foundation that will stand strong and endure the test as end-time storm winds begin to intensify.

In order to experience a revival of the Bible in your personal life, it is important to take time each day to read, receive, and apply its truths to your life. James tells us that if we will continue in the perfect law of liberty — refusing to be forgetful hearers, but determined to be doers — we will be blessed in our ways. As you watch or listen to the programs in this series and work through this corresponding study guide, I trust you will search the Scriptures and allow the Holy Spirit to help you hear something new from God's Word that applies specifically to your life. I encourage you to be a doer of the Word He reveals to you. Whatever the cost, I assure you — it will be worth it.

> Thy words were found, and I did eat them;
> and thy word was unto me the joy and rejoicing of mine heart:
> for I am called by thy name, O Lord God of hosts.
> — Jeremiah 15:16

Your brother and friend in Jesus Christ,

Rick Renner

Jesus Is Your Healer

Copyright © 2024 by Rick Renner
1814 W. Tacoma St.
Broken Arrow, OK 74012-1406

Published by Rick Renner Ministries
www.renner.org

ISBN 13: 978-1-6675-0636-4

ISBN 13 eBook: 978-1-6675-0637-1

The emphasis of this lesson:

God has pulled back the curtain on who Jesus is — and one of the most powerful revelations He has given us is that Jesus is our Healer! Through the work of redemption on the Cross, Jesus paid not only for our *sins* but for our *healing* too. His very nature is to heal. And through faith in Him, healing belongs to us!

The Power of Jesus' Sacrifice To Save and Heal

In her book *Jesus Is Your Healer*, Denise shares her heart that through the power of the Holy Spirit, you will fully understand and grab hold of the truth that Jesus is not just your Savior, but He is your Healer as well. Throughout the Bible, God reveals the power of His sacrifice both to save and to heal. Jesus is as much your Healer as He is your Savior!

You may be saying to yourself, *I already know that Jesus is my Savior and my Healer.* But consider this question: Are you *experiencing* Him as your Healer? This is an important question we all must ask ourselves. We hear sermons, read the Bible, and have head knowledge that Jesus is our Healer — we agree intellectually. But when sickness, disease, or pain comes to us or our loved ones, is our immediate response, "Jesus, You're my Healer"?

Let your faith for healing in your body arise as you look at the amazing truths and revelations that the Bible shows you about Jesus being your Savior *and* your Healer. (You can learn more about this powerful truth in Denise's book *Jesus Is Your Healer.*)

Pulling Back the Curtain on Jesus the Healer

God is so amazing! When He opens up revelation to us, it's like *He's pulling back a curtain.* Imagine a theater setting. As the curtain opens up little by little, we see more and more of what awaits us — first, a little part of the set decoration, then a little more, until we see the whole stage. This is what God has done in His Word when it comes to His healing and saving power. From the beginning of time, He opened up this revelation little by little.

In the Old Testament, the curtain is raised just a little bit, so we get only glimpses of Jesus being our Healer. There were two prophets who each raised a young man from the dead (*see* 1 Kings 17:17-24 and 2 Kings 4:32-37). In Numbers 12:10-15, we read about Miriam who was struck with leprosy, and

God removed the leprosy from her. Then there's Naaman, a Syrian general who came down with leprosy. He was given instructions by the prophet Elisha to go and dip in the river Jordan seven times, and Naaman was healed (*see* 2 Kings 5:1-14). The Old Testament also gives us an account of a king named Hezekiah who had behaved wickedly. But Hezekiah repented, and God extended his life an additional 15 years (*see* 2 Kings 20:1-6).

Little by little, through examples in Scripture verses, God is opening a curtain for us. We see this in Psalm 103:1-3 (*KJV*) an amazing passage of Scripture that says, "Bless the Lord, O my soul: and all that is within me, bless his holy name. Bless the Lord, O my soul, and forget not all his benefits: Who forgiveth all thine iniquities; *who healeth all thy diseases.*"

We see it clearly revealed in the Scriptures. God is pulling back the curtain on the powerful revelation that He is the forgiver of *all* iniquities (sins), and He is the Healer of *all* diseases (sicknesses). How many? Psalm 103 clearly says *all!* Is there an exception? No! He's the Healer! He's *your* Healer. And He is being exalted as your Healer as you study this revelation.

Jesus Paid a Mighty Price for Our Healing

Jesus gave His life on the Cross to also bring healing to you and me. God reveals in Psalm 103 that He is the forgiver of all sin and that He is the Healer of all diseases because of Jesus' work on the Cross. In Isaiah 53:4, it says, "Surely He has borne our griefs and carried our sorrows...."

The word "griefs" is translated from the Hebrew word meaning *sicknesses*. When Jesus was on the Cross, He bore on Himself all our sicknesses. He also carried our "sorrows," which is a translation from the Hebrew word that means *pain*. So if you're having pain in your body right now, Jesus bore — *lifted, carried, and took away* — that pain for you.

Denise experienced Jesus' mighty healing power, and shared one of her testimonies of healing on her program:

> Many, many years ago, I was pregnant with our second son, and I was getting so sick that I could not even keep down water. They found a medicine that would help me, and I began taking it, and things were going okay. Then as I was in my sixth month of pregnancy, my husband Rick began teaching about Jesus being our Healer. And I was listening, listening, and listening about what Jesus did on the Cross according to Isaiah 53.

I was listening and listening to the Word of God. And when you listen to the Word of God, faith arises in your heart. Well, one day faith arose in my heart, and I said to myself, "If Jesus took this sickness that I am having, why am *I* bearing it?" So I said, "I'm not taking that medicine tonight." (*Note:* Denise is *not* recommending you stop taking your medicine. This is just part of her testimony.)

I went to bed that night. At 3:00 a.m., I woke up and felt very sick, but as I lay in bed, I said, "No, I'm not taking this sickness. I'm not taking it because Jesus is my Healer, and He bore my pain and my sicknesses in His own body." And do you know what? I woke up the next morning, and I never had any problems again with being sick while being pregnant. And when I was pregnant with my third son, I was never sick. Why? Because I saw — not as just a Bible verse in my head — but I saw through faith, through revelation, that Jesus is not just my Savior, but He's my Healer.

Isaiah 53:4 says very clearly that Jesus bore our pains and took our sicknesses. That's so powerful! We all want our loved ones healed, and because of this verse, we have a way of bringing healing to them — by telling them what Jesus did! And they have a way of receiving that revelation and experiencing Him, not just as Jesus the Healer and the miracle worker in Matthew, Mark, Luke, John, and Acts, but as *their* Healer — *today*. He's *our* Healer — *right now*!

Through His death, burial, and resurrection, Jesus now reigns in Heaven. And the Bible says we're seated with Him there (*see* Ephesians 2:6 and Colossians 3:1)! He paid such a mighty price for us on the Cross because He wanted us to receive the fullness of how wonderful and powerful He is. He conquered *all* sickness and *all* disease on the Cross. We see this so plainly in Isaiah 53 in the Old Testament. But then Jesus came to the earth. God incarnate, inside of Jesus, came to the earth! What does this mean for our healing now?

Jesus Heals Because of His Compassion

At the start of Jesus' ministry, He walked into the temple, opened a scroll of the Scriptures, and read it. He said, "The Spirit of the Lord is upon Me, because He has anointed Me to preach the gospel to the poor; He has sent Me to heal the brokenhearted, to proclaim liberty to the captives and recovery of sight to the blind, to set at liberty those who are oppressed; to proclaim the acceptable year of the Lord" (Luke 4:18,19).

That day, Jesus proclaimed exactly who He was. He was anointed to open the sight of the blind, bring liberty to those who are oppressed, preach the gospel to the poor, and proclaim the acceptable year of the Lord. Once He announced who He was — and still is — Jesus began to display His power. And one of the first ways He displayed Himself to us was through His compassion.

Jesus *saw* the sick! He *saw* the hurting. In Luke 7:11-15, Jesus saw a woman in the midst of a funeral as they were burying her son. She was a widow, and this was her only son, and he had died. But Jesus saw her and had compassion on her. He said, in essence, "I'm going to interrupt that funeral." His compassion made Him the greatest interrupter!

The compassionate heart of God inside Jesus came forth for that woman. He walked over to the coffin, spoke to the young man, and raised him from the dead. Why did Jesus raise him from the dead? Was it just to perform a miracle? No! He did it because He had compassion on that mother, a widow.

Compassion is a powerful way that Jesus shows Himself as Healer. In the gospel of Mark, Jesus had compassion on a leper and healed him. Mark 1:40-42 says, "Now a leper came to Him, imploring Him, kneeling down to Him and saying to Him, 'If You are willing, You can make me clean.' Then Jesus, moved with compassion, stretched out His hand and touched him, and said to him, 'I am willing; be cleansed.' As soon as He had spoken, immediately the leprosy left him, and he was cleansed."

Jesus Heals Because of Our Faith

The Bible also reveals that Jesus showed Himself as Healer because people *believed* — it was their faith that led to their healing. Mark 5:25-34 contains the account of the woman who had an issue of blood (continual bleeding) for 12 years. Oh, how she suffered! The Bible says when she came through the crowd, she touched the hem of Jesus' garment. She broke all the religious rules to get to Jesus. Mark 5:27-29 says:

When she heard about Jesus, she came behind Him in the crowd and touched His garment. For she said, "If only I may

touch His clothes, I shall be made well." Immediately the fountain of her blood was dried up, and she felt in her body that she was healed of the affliction.

She wanted her act of faith to be a secret, but Jesus turned and asked the crowd, "Who touched Me?" He looked around for the person who touched Him. And the woman, trembling in fear, fell before Him. She began to tell Jesus everything. And do you know what Jesus said to her? He said, "Daughter, you are well because of your faith. Your *faith* made you well" (*see* Mark 5:34). Here we see Jesus can heal because of our faith. This is so powerful!

Jesus Heals Because He Wants To Heal

In Matthew 8, we read about another leper whom Jesus healed. In this instance, the leper came to Jesus saying, in essence, "I know that You can heal me." Perhaps he had heard about Jesus and the miracles He was doing. The leper worshiped Jesus, and he thought to himself, *I know that He can heal, but I don't know if he wants to heal ME.* Matthew 8:2 and 3 says:

> And behold, a leper came and worshiped Him, saying, "Lord, if You are willing, You can make me clean."

> Then Jesus put out His hand and touched him, saying, "I am willing; be cleansed." Immediately his leprosy was cleansed.

When the leper approached Jesus, the leper expressed what he was wondering. He said, in effect, "Jesus, I know You can heal me if You want to." And Jesus answered, "I *am* willing; be cleansed." Jesus laid His hand on the leper, and he was cleansed of the disease. In this simple reply, Jesus announced He is the compassionate Healer who *IS willing* to heal us! He wants us well!

Jesus Heals Because of His Own Faith

Isn't Jesus magnificent? As we consider these scriptures, the curtain is opening to reveal that Jesus is our Healer. We can see that Jesus heals with compassion, He heals because of one's faith in who He is, and He heals because it's His will to heal. And in the next scripture, we discover an instance when it was *Jesus'* faith that brought about healing.

Jesus' friend, Lazarus, had died, and nobody believed that Lazarus could be raised from the dead — *nobody*. Lazarus had been dead for four days, and no one, not even his sisters, believed that Jesus could raise him from the dead. John 11:43 and 44 says,

> **…He cried with a loud voice, "Lazarus, come forth!" And he who had died came out bound hand and foot with grave-clothes, and his face was wrapped with a cloth. Jesus said to them, "Loose him, and let him go."**

It was Jesus' faith that raised Lazarus from the dead. How powerful that is!

Jesus Heals Through His People

Jesus is not trying to keep healing *from* us — He's done everything to get healing *to* us. He's opening that curtain so we can see Him as our Healer and so others can see Him and know Him as their Healer as well. In Mark 16:18, Jesus said to those who believe in Him, "…They will lay hands on the sick, and they will recover." Jesus was saying to us, in effect, "I healed the sick. I moved in compassion. People were healed by their faith. Now *you* have Me — the Healer — inside you. Get your hands out of your pockets and lay them on the sick, and they will be healed."

Can you see the heart of God in Mark 16:18? His heart is so big that He wants to bring His healing power to us, so we can take His healing power to all who are sick. And in First Corinthians 12:7-10, the apostle Paul instructs us that we can be healed by a word of knowledge through the working of the Holy Spirit. We can be healed by gifts of healing or the working of miracles. Through these scriptures and others, we can see that Jesus is the express image of the Father (*see* Hebrews 1:3).

It is the Father's absolute will that we are healed. Jesus paid for our sickness — our part is to believe. We must believe that He is our Savior and our Healer, and He has compassion on *all* who are sick. And we must believe what Jesus endured on the Cross paid the price for us to be completely healed in our bodies.

By His Stripes, We Were Healed

God has totally opened the curtain to show us Jesus as Healer. First Peter 2:24 says, "Who Himself bore our sins in His own body on the tree, that we, having died to sins, might live for righteousness — by whose stripes you were healed." This verse was written by the apostle Peter who witnessed the chastisement and crucifixion of Jesus. Peter watched as our Savior was nailed to a cross.

When Jesus was scourged by the Roman soldiers with a cat-o'-nine-tails (a whip that had sharp metal objects on its tips), it cut deeply into His flesh, and He suffered greatly! Peter saw that. He saw the blood flowing from Jesus' body. And he said, "By His stripes, you *were* healed."

Jesus has already done it! He has already paid the price for your healing. He wants you to understand this so you can become renewed in your mind to know and believe the truth that He is your Healer. You don't have to live under the torment of sickness, disease, and pain. You don't have to be like the world and think that the answer is only found in the world when you get sick. You can receive the wonderful healing power that Jesus has made available to you through His death, burial, and resurrection.

Jesus is our Healer as much as He is our Savior. Yes, what He did on the Cross paid for our sins; by His blood, He has made us righteous in His sight. And we are healed by the stripes, the wounds, and the bruises that were put on Jesus for our sake when He went to the Cross. What a magnificent truth!

STUDY QUESTIONS

**Be diligent to present yourself approved to God, a worker
who does not need to be ashamed, rightly dividing the word of truth.
— 2 Timothy 2:15**

1. Compassion moved Jesus to action. Jesus *saw* the sick! He *saw* the hurting. He *saw* the widow of Nain in the middle of a funeral as they were burying her son (*see* Luke 7:11-15). Jesus *saw* her, had compassion on her, and raised her son from the dead. Just as Jesus saw those in need when He walked the earth, He sees you and *your* need today. Read Hebrews 12:2; Psalm 145:8 and 9; and Psalm 136:1. How is His love and compassion for you evident in these passages?

2. Romans 12:2 says, "…Be transformed by the renewing of your mind…." As you renew your mind to the tremendous truths in these lessons, realize that the Word of God is literally *transforming* you. Which healing scripture stands out to you personally? (*Consider* First Peter 2:24; Psalm 103:1-5; Isaiah 53:4 and 5; Psalm 107:20; and Matthew 8:17.)

3. In Mark 1:40-42, Jesus saw the leper, had compassion on him, and healed him. Notice that compassion *moved* Jesus to action. What should *our* response be when compassion rises up in our hearts toward someone who is hurting or sick? What can we do to help them? (*Consider* Mark 16:15-18.)

PRACTICAL APPLICATION

**But be doers of the word,
and not hearers only, deceiving yourselves.
—James 1:22**

1. Are you *experiencing* Jesus as your Healer? We may have head knowledge that Jesus is your Healer — you agree intellectually. But when sickness comes to you, is your immediate response, "Jesus, You're my Healer"? Rather than just agree intellectually, allow the truths in this lesson to get inside your heart. Take time to write down the healing scriptures that stand out to you and meditate on them. "So then faith comes by hearing, and hearing by the word of God" (Romans 10:17).

2. Jesus bore your pains and He took your sicknesses. He paid the price for you to be completely healed in your body. Jesus is not trying to keep healing *from* you — He did everything to get it *to* you. If you need healing in your body right now, receive that wonderful healing power that Jesus has made available to you through His death, burial, and resurrection. The power of the Holy Spirit is present to remove pain *right now* because Jesus carried your pains. His power is present to remove sickness *right now* because He took your sickness. Are you thankful for His finished work on the Cross? Shout, "Thank You, Lord, for healing me! By Your stripes, I was healed!"

3. Psalm 103:1-3 (*KJV*) says, "Bless the Lord, O my soul: and all that is within me, bless his holy name. Bless the Lord, O my soul, and forget not all his benefits: Who forgiveth all thine iniquities; who healeth all thy diseases." Take note of how you are instructed to bless the Lord with all that is within you. Notice the repetition in this passage's admonition to bless the Lord. He saved you! He healed you! When was the last time you blessed the Lord — *with all that is within you* — for saving you? Take time to do that now. And then, bless the Lord — *with all that is within you* — for healing you. Hallelujah! There is power in heartfelt praise!

TOPIC

Faith Stands Still

SCRIPTURES

1. **James 1:6-8** — But let him ask in faith, with no doubting, for he who doubts is like a wave of the sea driven and tossed by the wind. For let not that man suppose that he will receive anything from the Lord; he is a double-minded man, unstable in all his ways.

2. **Mark 10:46-52** — Now they came to Jericho. As He went out of Jericho with His disciples and a great multitude, blind Bartimaeus, the son of Timaeus, sat by the road begging. And when he heard that it was Jesus of Nazareth, he began to cry out and say, "Jesus, Son of David, have mercy on me!" Then many warned him to be quiet; but he cried out all the more, "Son of David, have mercy on me!" So Jesus stood still and commanded him to be called. Then they called the blind man, saying to him, "Be of good cheer. Rise, He is calling you." And throwing aside his garment, he rose and came to Jesus. So Jesus answered and said to him, "What do you want Me to do for you?" The blind man said to Him, "Rabboni, that I may receive my sight." Then Jesus said to him, "Go your way; your faith has made you well." And immediately he received his sight and followed Jesus on the road.

3. **Hebrews 11:6** — But without faith it is impossible to please Him, for he who comes to God must believe that He is, and that He is a rewarder of those who diligently seek Him.

4. **1 John 5:4** — For whatever is born of God overcomes the world. And this is the victory that has overcome the world — our faith.

SYNOPSIS

As we believe God for healing, it's important to understand that faith is a real place where we must stand firm. We see this in the healing of blind Bartimaeus — who heard Jesus the Healer was coming, cried out for mercy, ignored the doubting crowd, and cast off his beggar's garment. His faith changed his identity — from a blind man to a man who could see! Likewise, as we stand unwavering in faith, miracles of healing can be ours.

The emphasis of this lesson:

Often, receiving our healing or believing for the healing of a loved one requires us to stand firm in our faith — refusing to be moved, regardless of circumstances and the opinions of others. Rather than letting doubt creep in and block our miracle, we must stand firm, trusting that our faith will make us well.

Stand Fast in Your Faith for Healing

In lesson 1, we focused on the power of Jesus' sacrifice on the Cross both to save and to heal. In today's lesson, we will see the power of holding on to our faith in Jesus and what He did for us on the Cross. Many times when we believe for our healing, or we are believing for somebody else's healing, it is a real fight of faith.

It's important to know that faith is a real place, and we must stand still in that place of faith! We must not let faith get away from us! We must continually renew our minds to what Jesus did for us on the Cross. His finished work on the Cross paid for our redemption — and this includes healing.

Why must we renew our minds? We renew our minds to keep ourselves aligned with the truth of God's Word and to easily recognize thoughts that don't agree with His Word. Day and night, the devil is accusing us before the Lord (*see* Revelation 12:10), and in this world, this accuser is walking about, looking for those whom he may devour (*see* 1 Peter 5:8). This world is perverse. But God has given us His power inside us so we can be a light in this world. Believing Him and standing fast in our faith and the Word of God is a way that we can shine.

'Hope Came Into My Heart'

On her program, Denise shared that God has healed her body, and her testimony has been a tremendous encouragement to others. She shared the following testimony of healing as an encouragement to you:

> For 13 years, I suffered with a disease on my face, and it wasn't just a "teenage" problem. I had sores that went into all five layers of my skin — on my neck, cheeks, and forehead. It was painful, and it was ugly. Year after year, I went to the doctors and took

their medicine. And then one day, I heard a preacher on the radio say, "By His stripes, you are healed."

I loved Jesus, but I had never heard that I had been healed by the stripes He had taken on His body when He was crucified. And when I heard it, hope came into my heart. When you have a disease or a problem for a long time, you think, *This is just my lot in life*. No! Not with what Jesus did for us! I just didn't have that revelation before.

But when I heard that preacher say, "By the stripes of Jesus, you are healed," hope came into my heart. I said to myself, *You mean I can be healed? I've looked in the mirror for 13 years. I have been to the doctors. I have taken their medicine. I have been in pain. I have had bruises on my face. You mean I could be healed?*

At that point, an expectancy came into my heart, and I began to confess God's Word. I did not see anything immediately, but my faith was rooted in the truth of His Word. And a few months later I had my miracle. I went to bed one night with that disease, just like I had for 13 years, and I woke up the next morning without it — my complexion was completely clean.

Everything — the sores, the bruising, the pain — was gone; gone from my neck, my cheeks, and my forehead. I'd had so much infection in my face and my neck that after my healing, people thought I'd lost ten pounds. I don't know if Jesus took five minutes or all night, but I know that sometime during that night, His miracle-working power overcame the disease that had been on me for 13 years. I woke up the next morning completely healed. So I have a conviction in my heart about Jesus being my Healer — my Savior *and* my Healer.

Stand in Faith on What You Hear

By faith, we know that Jesus is not only our Savior but our Healer. But when we are in a real fight, we must *stand still* with our faith. What does that mean? James 1:6-8 says, "But let him ask in faith, with no doubting, for he who doubts is like a wave of the sea driven and tossed by the wind. For let not that man suppose that he will receive anything from the Lord; he is a double-minded man, unstable in all his ways." We can't be like a wave on the sea that's tossed by the wind. We must *stand still* with our faith.

There's an amazing example of a man in the Bible whose faith stood still — blind Bartimaeus. His story begins in Mark 10:46: "Now they came to Jericho. As He [Jesus] went out of Jericho with His disciples and a great multitude, blind Bartimaeus, the son of Timaeus, sat by the road begging."

We don't know how blind Bartimaeus heard about Jesus, but there sat Bartimaeus — by the road and begging. Mark 10:47 says, "And when he heard that it was Jesus of Nazareth, he began to cry out and say, 'Jesus, Son of David, have mercy on me!'"

Of course, blind Bartimaeus couldn't see Jesus, and we don't know how he heard that Jesus was nearby, but we know that he heard. Maybe people were saying, "Make way! It's Jesus of Nazareth. Jesus is coming! He's healed the sick. Blind eyes have been opened. I know a man who couldn't walk, and He healed him. Get out of the way — Jesus is coming!"

'Have Mercy on Me!'

Blind Bartimaeus responded to what he heard, and he immediately called out to Jesus, "Son of David, have mercy on me!" (v. 48) The Bible says that Bartimaeus didn't just say this once. He said it over and over and over again. He cried out for mercy.

As the crowd around Bartimaeus screamed and yelled, they told him to be quiet. We can just imagine what they must have said: "Oh, blind Bartimaeus, you've been in that spot ever since I've known you. You've sat there begging every single day. You're dirty. You're stinky. You're just a blind beggar, so forget it. Be quiet, Bartimaeus. You're too loud. Jesus is not going to pay attention to you."

The Bible says the crowd severely warned blind Bartimaeus, but did that stop him from crying out to Jesus? No! God's Word says that "he cried out all the more" (v. 48). Their negative words did not stop blind Bartimaeus. Their opinions didn't move him from his place of faith. Bartimaeus' faith stood still.

Refuse To Be Moved by Negative Opinions

Maybe you're fighting sickness or maybe someone you love is fighting pain. You are believing for healing, but others around you don't have the faith to believe. You are speaking words of life and truth, and they are speaking their opinion — and it's not faith. Does this sound familiar? On the program, Denise shared a testimony of being in that situation:

> A similar experience happened to me recently. I was in a place of believing for my friend's healing. She was not in good condition, and the doctor said she only had a 50-percent chance of living. People around me said, "Denise, you just need to get used to it because she's not going to make it through this."
>
> And I said, "Of course, she's going to make it through this!" And do you know what? My friend is walking around today, and she is doing very well. That disease is no longer in her body. If we had given up — if I hadn't stood still by my faith and if she hadn't stood still by her faith — I don't know where she would be right now.

Faith has to stand still against the thoughts and opinions of other people. And blind Bartimaeus was in that very situation. He had to stand still with his faith and not care what anybody else was saying. Instead, Bartimaeus remained focused on Jesus, the Son of David, having mercy on him and giving him his sight. And no one was going to stop him.

Jesus Stood Still and Called the Blind Man

Jesus must have heard blind Bartimaeus calling out to Him for mercy. Mark 10:49 continues, "So Jesus stood still and commanded him to be called." Not only does our faith stand still, but our faith touches God — and it moves Him to respond. Hebrews 11:6 says, "But without faith it is impossible to please Him, for he who comes to God must believe that He is, and that He is a rewarder of those who diligently seek Him."

Blind Bartimaeus did not give up asking for what he wanted from Jesus, even though everybody was sharing their opinion and trying to get him to shut up. As a result of Bartimaeus's faith, Jesus stood still and commanded blind Bartimaeus to be called to Him. Bartimaeus had Jesus' attention, and now the crowd supported him: "Be of good cheer. Rise, He is calling you" (v. 49).

Some people genuinely care about us, but when most people speak about a situation, they're usually just expressing their opinion. And if the wind changes, then their opinion is going to change as well — like the crowd that surrounded Bartimaeus. First, they rebuked him and told him to shut up. Then when Jesus called for blind Bartimaeus, they cheered him on.

Maybe we've listened to the opinions of others, which may have caused us to doubt or give up our convictions — even though opinions can change the next day or the next minute. We must stand still in our faith in God's Word, and not let the opinions of others have any impact on us. Blind Bartimaeus ignored the roaring sea of opinions. Mark 10:50 says, "And throwing aside his garment, he rose and came to Jesus."

Faith Will Change Your Identity

That garment that Bartimaeus tossed aside represented his identity as a blind beggar — it was his meal ticket. It gave him the right to sit in that same place outside Jericho every day and beg for money. But these verses of scripture tell us that when Jesus called out, blind Bartimaeus took off that garment and threw it aside.

First, Bartimaeus' faith stood still. Then Jesus stood still. And then Bartimaeus stood in front of Jesus, and Jesus said to him, "What do you want Me to do for you?" (Mark 10:51)

Have you ever considered why Jesus said that? Surely He knew what Bartimaeus wanted. He must have known the blind man wanted his sight. But here we see how important it is that we say — speak out of our mouth — what it is we want the Lord to do for us.

Faith must be involved to receive our healing. Faith has to stand still to receive from God, and we see a tremendous example of this in blind Bartimaeus. Blindness had been his identity. Every day he went to that exact spot and begged. But when he heard that Jesus was passing by, Bartimaeus's faith stood still. He cried out to Jesus, and he ignored the jeers of the crowd. He threw aside his garment — his identity as a blind beggar and his source of income — and approached Jesus. Bartimaeus didn't need that garment anymore because he wasn't going to be blind anymore! Faith changed his identity. And faith will change your identity.

Bartimaeus' story concludes, "So Jesus answered him [Bartimaeus] and said to him, 'What do you want Me to do for you?' The blind man said to Him, 'Rabboni, that I may receive my sight.' Then Jesus said to him, 'Go your way; your faith has made you well.' And immediately he received his sight and followed Jesus on the road" (Mark 10:51,52).

Don't Underestimate Your Faith!

Jesus acknowledged *Bartimaeus' faith* — faith that stood still to receive what he was believing for. Don't underestimate your faith! First John 5:4 says, "For whatever is born of God overcomes the world. And this is the victory that has overcome the world — our faith." We overcome in this world by *our faith*. And faith works "through love" (*see* Galatians 5:6). So we don't want to give up on our faith. No! Faith is a real place, and we can't move away from it. We must stand still in our faith and receive what we are asking for.

Again, James 1:6-8 admonishes, "But let him ask in faith, with no doubting, for he who doubts is like a wave of the sea driven and tossed by the wind. For let not that man suppose that he will receive anything from the Lord; he is a double-minded man, unstable in all his ways." We don't want that to be us! We want Jesus to look at us and say, "They are standing in faith. They believe me. Their faith is opening the door for what I've done for them."

Don't stop believing God! Regardless of the circumstances surrounding you — whether it's financial, relational, physical, or somebody else's need for a miracle — stay in the place of faith. Jesus paid a great price, and He wants you to have everything that He paid for. Stand still in your faith and believe God for what He has promised you.

STUDY QUESTIONS

Be diligent to present yourself approved to God, a worker who does not need to be ashamed, rightly dividing the word of truth.
— 2 Timothy 2:15

1. It matters what we do in the midst of the fight of faith. The opinions of others may conflict with your stance of faith, and you may even need to contend with your own thoughts. What should you do if your thoughts aren't aligned with the Word of God? (*Consider* Second Corinthians 10:5; Philippians 4:8; and Joshua 1:8.)

2. Regardless of the challenges you may encounter, what does the Bible promise? (*Consider* First Corinthians 15:57; First John 4:4; and Romans 8:37.)

3. Don't underestimate the power of your faith! What did the individuals in the following passages receive by faith? (*Consider* Matthew 9:20-22; Mark 10:51,52; and Luke 7:1-10.)

PRACTICAL APPLICATION

But be doers of the word,
and not hearers only, deceiving yourselves.
— James 1:22

1. In Mark 10:50, we see what Bartimaeus did when Jesus commanded him to be called: "And throwing aside his garment, he rose and came to Jesus." Notice that three things happened:

   • He *threw aside his garment* — which represented his identity.

   • He *rose* from a seated position. Previously, he "sat by the road begging" (*see* v. 46).

   • He *came to Jesus*. He responded to the Master's word and went to Jesus, the Healer.

   What do you need to *throw off*? What do you need to *rise up* and *go to Jesus* about?

2. Faith doesn't quit. Just as we saw in the story of blind Bartimaeus, faith cries out, stands amidst opposition, and *receives* from Jesus. Jesus asked Bartimaeus, "What do you want Me to do for you?" (Mark 10:51). If Jesus asked you what He asked Bartimaeus, what would you say? Take time to get into the presence of the Lord and let Him know specifically what you need, then let your faith stand still.

3. Take time to meditate on the following aspects of faith that we've learned from this lesson.

   • Faith pleases God. (*Consider* Hebrews 11:6.)

   • Faith makes you well. (*Consider* Mark 10:52.)

   • Faith overcomes the world. (*Consider* First John 5:4.)

   • Faith stands firm against opposing opinions of others. (*Consider* Mark 10:48.)

   • Faith touches God and moves Him to respond. (*Consider* Hebrews 11:6.)

TOPIC

Faith That Overcomes the Impossible

SCRIPTURES

1. **Matthew 15:21-28** — Then Jesus went out from there and departed to the region of Tyre and Sidon. And behold, a woman of Canaan came from that region and cried out to Him, saying, "Have mercy on me, O Lord, Son of David! My daughter is severely demon-possessed." But He answered her not a word. And His disciples came and urged Him, saying, "Send her away, for she cries out after us." But He answered and said, "I was not sent except to the lost sheep of the house of Israel." Then she came and worshiped Him, saying, "Lord, help me!" But He answered and said, "It is not good to take the children's bread and throw it to the little dogs." And she said, "Yes, Lord, yet even the little dogs eat the crumbs which fall from their masters' table." Then Jesus answered and said to her, "O woman, great is your faith! Let it be to you as you desire." And her daughter was healed from that very hour.

2. **John 6:51** — "I am the living bread which came down from heaven. If anyone eats of this bread, he will live forever; and the bread that I shall give is My flesh, which I shall give for the life of the world."

SYNOPSIS

Jesus came to heal *all* — and our faith in Him can move even the most impossible mountain to bring us healing. We find a beautiful example of this mountain-moving faith in the story of the Canaanite woman whose daughter was demon-possessed (*see* Matthew 15). Though obstacle after obstacle stood in her way, she kept her faith in Jesus, even worshiping Him in her time of great need, and her daughter was healed. Likewise, as we stand firm in our faith and worship Jesus, He responds with His healing power to set us free.

The emphasis of this lesson:

Your faith and your worship touch the heart of God and open the door for your miracle! When obstacles arise, press into God. Stay firm in

your faith, worship Him, call out to the Living Bread — Jesus — and expect your miracle to come.

Many people know Jesus as their Savior, but He wants to reveal Himself as our Healer too. It is so important to renew our mind to this truth! Yes, we must know Jesus as our Lord and Savior, but we must also know Him as our Healer.

Let's look at a woman who pushed through many obstacles to receive healing in her time of need. Her faith was tenacious, and she would not give up. Likewise, there are often obstacles that we must press through to receive the healing that is ours, and we don't want to let them stop us from receiving everything that Jesus purchased for us on the Cross.

A Woman Cries Out for Her Daughter's Deliverance

The account of the Canaanite woman is found in Matthew 15:21-28. Let's take a look at what these scriptures tell us about her — and how she pushed through obstacle after obstacle to receive a miracle from Jesus the Healer!

> Then Jesus went out from there and departed to the region of Tyre and Sidon. And behold, a woman of Canaan came from that region and cried out to Him, saying, "Have mercy on me, O Lord, Son of David! My daughter is severely demon-possessed." But He answered her not a word. And His disciples came and urged Him, saying, "Send her away, for she cries out after us." But He answered and said, "I was not sent except to the lost sheep of the house of Israel."
>
> Then she came and worshiped Him, saying, "Lord, help me!" But He answered and said, "It is not good to take the children's bread and throw it to the little dogs." And she said, "Yes, Lord, yet even the little dogs eat the crumbs which fall from their masters' table." Then Jesus answered and said to her, "O woman, great is your faith! Let it be to you as you desire." And her daughter was healed from that very hour.

During this time period, Jews and Canaanites typically did not get along, and the Canaanites — known as a corrupt and violent culture — certainly were not in covenant with God. But this did not stop this Canaanite woman from coming to Jesus and crying out for mercy. In the original Greek translation, it denotes that she didn't just cry out once — she cried out *many times.*

Seek His Mercy in Desperate Situations

This Canaanite woman was asking Jesus for mercy and to deliver her daughter who was severely demon-possessed. Maybe you have a child or a spouse who is addicted to drugs or alcohol, and you've witnessed the suffering and torment this person is going through. You may worry or even cry because you're so broken by the whole situation.

When the enemy attacks or a serious situation happens to someone you love, it weighs on you. Watching as oppression or an addiction overtakes a loved one hurts you — and you cry out. That's what was happening to this woman. She cried out for God's mercy for her demon-possessed daughter.

In the Bible, demon possession is often described by referring to the various ways a person was afflicted or stricken. The tormented person may have had convulsions (*see* Luke 9:42), or the demon may have tried to throw the afflicted person into the fire or the water (*see* Mark 9:22). In Mark 5:5, a demon-possessed man cut himself with stones. But in Matthew 15:22, the Canaanite woman described her daughter as "severely demon-possessed," so we don't know which or how many of those attributes she had, but it must have been overwhelming.

This mother was desperate to help her daughter. And when she saw Jesus, the first thing she did was cry out to the Lord. Over and over, she called out to Jesus, "Have mercy on me, O Lord, Son of David! My daughter is severely demon-possessed" (Matthew 15:22).

Faith Refuses To Give Up

The Bible says that Jesus "answered her not a word" (v. 23). That must have been hard enough for her to experience, but then the disciples said, "Send her away, for she cries out after us" (Matthew 15:23). In essence, they were complaining, "She's bothering us, Lord. Send her away."

From the woman's point of view, the situation must have seemed hopeless. First, Jesus ignored her, and then the disciples asked Jesus to send her away. And then Jesus spoke. But He said, "I was not sent except to the lost sheep of the house of Israel" (Matthew 15:24).

After hearing those words, the woman could have given up. She could have said, "Okay, Jesus. I'm in the wrong place. I don't know what to do about my daughter, but I can tell that You're not going to help me." But not this woman! She would not give up because she had faith. She believed that Jesus was going to do something to help her daughter. Her faith in Him was powerful!

Stand on the Word of God

Our faith in Jesus is powerful, especially when we stand on His Word to receive our healing. As we meditate on the truth of God's Word, we can stay in a place of peace because we *know* and *believe* that "by His stripes we are healed" (*see* Isaiah 53:5).

On her program, Denise shared the testimony of a friend who faced obstacles — and whose faith brought her through to her miracle.

> Many years ago, my friend was diagnosed with a terrible brain tumor. And it wasn't contained — it had spread to different places. She was going to have surgery, and they didn't have very much hope for her. But she was holding on to the Word of God that the resurrection power of God lived in her (*see* Romans 8:11).
>
> She wasn't worried as she went into surgery. In fact, she told me she was laughing because she was thinking about the power of God in her. The doctor went in and operated on her. Then he came back to her husband, and he had an unusual look on his face. The doctor said, "We operated on your wife, and when we opened her up, there were no tumors."
>
> Hallelujah! You see, the obstacles were there. The bad reports from the doctors were there. I'm sure they saw things on the X-rays and all the tests that they did. But my friend was standing on the Word of God.

Likewise, this Canaanite woman was standing on her faith in Jesus. She was not giving up. Even though Jesus had just said, "I wasn't sent to you, but only to the lost sheep of Israel," she didn't go away. She continued to believe. She kept throwing herself on the mercy of the Lord, crying out to Him even more.

Worship and Faith Touch the Heart of God

Faith is powerful, and worship is powerful too! Matthew 15:25 says, "…She [the Canaanite woman] came and worshiped Him, saying, 'Lord, help me!'"

The Bible mentions other people whom God delivered because they worshipped Him — those who believed! Do you remember the Hebrew young men — Shadrach, Meshach, and Abed-Nego? They faced a fiery furnace that had been turned up seven times hotter than usual because they refused to worship King Nebuchadnezzar's gods (*see* Daniel 3:19). The Hebrew men said, in essence, "Oh, king, we hear your command. We hear what you're saying to us. But we will not bow before your image. Our God can deliver us. And even if He doesn't deliver us, we're not going to bow to your gods" (*see* Daniel 3:16-18). That's great worship before the Lord!

Shadrach, Meshach, and Abed-Nego were bound and thrown into the fiery furnace, but they weren't in there alone. Astonished, the king said, "Look!…I see four men loose, walking in the midst of the fire; and they are not hurt, and the form of the fourth is like the Son of God" (v. 25). The fourth man in the fire was Jesus! When we worship God — when we open our heart and believe God, no matter what we're facing — our faith and our worship touch the heart of God.

Worship Overcomes Obstacles

In Acts 16, we find another account of worship touching God's heart. The apostle Paul and Silas had been beaten and thrown into prison with their feet fastened in stocks because they were preaching the Gospel. Acts 16:25 and 26 says, "But at midnight Paul and Silas were praying and singing hymns to God, and the prisoners were listening to them. Suddenly there was a great earthquake, so that the foundations of the prison were shaken; and immediately all the doors were opened and everyone's chains were loosed"

What did Paul and Silas' singing and praising God do? It brought an earthquake right to their jail cell, loosed their bonds, and freed them from that prison. Worship is powerful!

In Second Chronicles 20, we read about the Israelite army that was outnumbered by three enemy armies. Did the Israelites give up or surrender? No! They went down to face those enemies, and they started worshiping

God. They sang and declared, "Praise the Lord, for His mercy endures forever" (2 Chronicles 20:21). And as they sang and praised the Lord, the Lord set ambushes against their enemies, and the enemy armies destroyed each other (*see* v. 22)!

That is the power of worship. And this is what the Canaanite woman did on behalf of her daughter — she worshiped the Lord. We don't know what her worship looked like. Some scholars say that she threw herself on the ground. Her prayer was sincere, direct, and short. Matthew 15:25 reveals, "Then she came and worshiped Him, saying, 'Lord, help me.'"

How did Jesus respond to her simple, heartfelt prayer for help? He said, "It's not good to take the children's bread and throw it to the little dogs" (v. 26). But even this rebuke did not deter her. Standing still in her faith, she said, "Yes, Lord, yet even the little dogs eat the crumbs which fall from their masters' table" (Matthew 15:27).

'Just Give Me a Crumb'

Jesus' words sound harsh, but when the Canaanite woman was refused over and over again and the Lord referred to her as a dog, He wasn't demeaning her — it was just the attitude of that culture at that time. And the woman said, in essence, "Okay, I accept that. I agree that I'm not worthy of the covenant of the children of Israel — but I don't need the whole loaf."

When Jesus mentioned "the children's bread," she was thinking of the bread on the table. She thought, *There are crumbs that fall off the table, and little dogs eat the crumbs that end up on the floor. He just reckoned me as a dog, and I don't disagree with that, but the little dogs get to eat the crumbs.* She was saying to Him, in effect, "I don't have to have the whole loaf. Just give me one of those crumbs when it falls from the children's bread of healing. All I need is a little crumb."

What humility and faith this Canaanite woman displayed in her response to Jesus! Her daughter wasn't even present that day, but the desperate mother was ready to receive the girl's deliverance at Jesus' word. This Gentile woman understood that there was as much healing power in the crumbs as there was in the loaf of bread.

One Word Is All We Need

The woman's response revealed what she believed about Jesus, and it was the response of faith that He always listened for. Verse 28 says, "Then Jesus answered and said to her, 'O woman, great is your faith! Let it be to you as you desire.' And her daughter was healed from that very hour." One word from Jesus was all the woman needed, and all she desired to hear. That's the word we want to hear from Jesus as well — "Let it be done as you desire."

Sometimes we give up too quickly. But not this Canaanite mother! She was rejected over and over again, but she kept pressing in and stood still in her faith. She knew she might be seen as a dog in that culture, but she persisted and said, in essence, "Even the dogs are given the crumbs from the table. Please, Lord, help me. You don't have to give me the whole loaf. You can give that to your children, but just give me a crumb." How powerful is that!

The Canaanite woman's story is a picture of what can happen when someone believes God's Word about healing over a diagnosis of cancer. This person sees the doctor's dire prognosis, but he or she trusts God's Word as the final authority concerning his or her healing. This person believes like the Canaanite woman did — maybe his or her faith for healing isn't for a whole loaf. Maybe it's just for a crumb.

Why are we talking about crumbs? Because the devil is a liar, and sometimes he may say, "You're not *worthy* of being healed," or, in other words, "You don't deserve the whole loaf." But to the Canaanite woman, there was as much power in a crumb as there was in a whole loaf. And like her, we can declare, "Then I'll take a crumb, because in the crumb there is as much power as there is in the healing loaf."

Jesus Is the Healing Bread

In John 6:51, Jesus said, "I am the living bread which came down from heaven. If anyone eats of this bread, he will live forever; and the bread that I shall give is My flesh, which I shall give for the life of the world." When Jesus sacrificed Himself — His flesh — on the Cross, He gave us salvation; He gave us deliverance; He opened the doors of Heaven to us so we would not have to languish in hell forever and ever. And He gave us healing, so we wouldn't have to be tormented by sickness and disease on this side of Heaven.

He's as much your Healer as He is your Savior. Like the Canaanite woman, you *can* receive from Jesus — the Living Bread — all the healing you need. The woman's faith would not quit. She received only a crumb, but in that crumb was the same power that was in the whole loaf of bread, and her daughter was healed.

Jesus is offering you the healing bread right now. Whatever you need in *your* fight of faith — whether it's healing in your body, mind, relationships, or healing for a loved one — stay in faith. Stand still in your faith, and don't give up. Your faith and worship are powerful, and they can and will overcome the impossible!

STUDY QUESTIONS

Be diligent to present yourself approved to God, a worker
who does not need to be ashamed, rightly dividing the word of truth.
— 2 Timothy 2:15

1. When the three Hebrew young men were thrown into the fiery furnace, there was a fourth man in the fire with them — it was Jesus! (*See* Daniel 3:19-25.) Know that whatever fiery test you are going through, you are not alone; Jesus is with you. And He will deliver you just like He delivered Shadrach, Meshach, and Abed-nego! What did God promise us regarding His presence during times of trouble? (*Consider* Isaiah 43:1,2; Hebrews 13:5 (*AMPC*); Psalm 46:1,2; and Psalm 91:15,16.)

2. When Jesus gave His flesh, He gave healing. When He gave His flesh, He gave deliverance. When He gave His flesh, He gave salvation and opened the doors of Heaven to you. He took the stripes on His back so that you wouldn't have to be tormented by sickness and disease. Jesus is as much your Healer as He is your Savior. Take a moment to write down the following scriptures or underline them in your Bible: Isaiah 53:4,5; Psalm 103:1-5; and First Peter 2:24. What words do you see repeated in these scriptures?

3. Humility and faith go hand-in-hand. Notice the Canaanite woman's persistent faith, but also notice her posture of humility in the midst of her stance of faith (see Matthew 15:21-28). She humbly submitted to

the Master while holding on to faith for her urgent need. When Jesus spoke of "the children's bread," she humbly asked for a crumb — and she got it! What do the following Scriptures teach us about humility? *See* James 4:6; Philippians 2:3-11; and First Peter 5:5.

PRACTICAL APPLICATION

But be doers of the word,
and not hearers only, deceiving yourselves.
— James 1:22

1. Mark 15:34 tells us what Jesus said as He hung on the Cross. "At the ninth hour Jesus cried out with a loud voice, saying, 'Eloi, Eloi, lama sabachthani?' which is translated, 'My God, My God, why have You forsaken Me?'" Jesus was forsaken in His *worst* moment so you would never be forsaken in yours. He is the God who "will never leave you nor forsake you" (*see* Hebrews 13:5). Take a moment now to get quiet before Him and sincerely acknowledge His presence. Meditate on the truth that you are *not forsaken*, even in your most difficult moments.

2. In the midst of her desperate need, the Canaanite woman "came and worshiped Him…" (Matthew 15:25). Are you facing a difficult situation? Take time to worship God. Worship touches His heart. It's an expression of faith. Abraham was "strengthened in faith, giving glory to God, and being fully convinced that what He had promised He was also able to perform" (Romans 4:20,21). You may not *feel* like it, but by faith, lift your heart, your eyes, and your hands to Him, and sincerely *worship* Him.

3. In Matthew 15:25, the woman cried out, "Lord, help me!" Her prayer was only three words long, but it got results! God isn't looking for lengthy religious prayers. You are His child, and you can come to Him as your Father and simply ask for what you need and receive from Him. Take a moment to simply ask God for exactly what you need.

TOPIC

Jesus Is Both Savior and Healer

SCRIPTURES

1. **Psalm 103:2,3** — Bless the Lord, O my soul, and forget not all His benefits: Who forgives all your iniquities, Who heals all your diseases.

2. **Isaiah 53:4,5** — Surely He has borne our griefs and carried our sorrows; yet we esteemed Him stricken, smitten by God, and afflicted. But He was wounded for our transgressions, He was bruised for our iniquities; the chastisement for our peace was upon Him, and by His stripes we are healed.

3. **Mark 2:2-12** — Immediately many gathered together, so that there was no longer room to receive them, not even near the door. And He preached the word to them. Then they came to Him, bringing a paralytic who was carried by four men. And when they could not come near Him because of the crowd, they uncovered the roof where He was. So when they had broken through, they let down the bed on which the paralytic was lying. When Jesus saw their faith, He said to the paralytic, "Son, your sins are forgiven you." And some of the scribes were sitting there and reasoning in their hearts, "Why does this Man speak blasphemies like this? Who can forgive sins but God alone?" But immediately, when Jesus perceived in His spirit that they reasoned thus within themselves, He said to them, "Why do you reason about these things in your hearts? Which is easier, to say to the paralytic, 'Your sins are forgiven you,' or to say, 'Arise, take up your bed and walk'? But that you may know that the Son of Man has power on earth to forgive sins" — He said to the paralytic, "I say to you, arise, take up your bed, and go to your house." Immediately he arose, took up the bed, and went out in the presence of them all, so that all were amazed and glorified God, saying, "We never saw anything like this!"

4. **Matthew 8:16** — When evening had come, they brought to Him many who were demon-possessed. And He cast out the spirits with a word, and healed all who were sick.

5. **Matthew 14:14** — And when Jesus went out He saw a great multitude; and He was moved with compassion for them, and healed their sick.

6. **Matthew 19:2** — And great multitudes followed Him, and He healed them there.

7. **Matthew 21:14** — Then the blind and the lame came to Him in the temple, and He healed them.

8. **Matthew 12:15** — But when Jesus knew it, He withdrew from there. And great multitudes followed Him, and He healed them all.

9. **Acts 10:38** — How God anointed Jesus of Nazareth with the Holy Spirit and with power, who went about doing good and healing all who were oppressed by the devil, for God was with Him.

SYNOPSIS

Persistence in faith is essential to receiving our healing. This truth is evident in the story of the paralytic, whose friends lowered him through the roof to receive a miracle of healing from the Lord. Their faith interrupted Jesus, who then stopped what He was doing in order to declare the man's sins forgiven and his body healed. In doing so, Jesus revealed God's heart for us — that we would be both saved and healed by the finished work of Jesus on the Cross.

The emphasis of this lesson:

Jesus took *all* our sins and healed *all* our diseases — He is both Savior *and* Healer. As we renew our mind to this truth, we strengthen our faith to receive His healing power, just as we have faith to receive His gift of salvation.

He Heals All Your Diseases

It's in Second Samuel 11 in the Old Testament where we read of the sin committed by King David. There were grave consequences for his poor choices, but God gave David a clear revelation of His love and mercy, and it brought David to a place of repentance. In Psalm 103:2 and 3, David wrote, "Bless the Lord, O my soul, and forget not all His benefits: Who forgives all your iniquities, Who heals all your diseases." David knew he was forgiven, and he knew he was healed.

Isaiah 53:4 says, "Surely He has borne our griefs and carried our sorrows; yet we esteemed Him stricken, smitten by God, and afflicted." The word "sorrows" here is a translation of a Hebrew word, which means *pains*. If you have pain in your body, Jesus already carried it on Himself to the Cross for you. Isaiah 53:5 goes on to say, "But He was wounded for our transgressions, He was bruised for our iniquities; the chastisement for our peace was upon Him, and by His stripes we are healed."

Jesus paid the highest price to purchase your healing! You might be saying, "You know, I'm not very spiritual, and I don't read my Bible enough," or "I don't tithe, and I'm not very good to people, so this must not apply to me." Yes, it would be good if you tithed and read your Bible and treated people kindly, but that does not change His love for you or what He did *for you*.

Jesus loves you, and His healing power is for you as much as it is for someone you think is doing everything "right." God "shows no partiality" (*see* Acts 10:34). In the *King James Version*, it says that He's "no respecter of persons." He doesn't play favorites, and He loves you completely — just as you are. He's so wonderful!

Persistent Faith Pays Off!

Let's look at a powerful story of persistence and faith for healing found in the gospel of Mark. Jesus was teaching a large crowd of people in Capernaum. Beginning in verse 2, it says, "Immediately many gathered together, so that there was no longer room to receive them, not even near the door. And He preached the word to them." The writer of this gospel noted that so many people had come to this house to hear Jesus speak that there was no more room for anyone else to fit inside. The people in attendance were crammed together — even in the doorway.

Mark 2:3 and 4 goes on to say, "Then they came to Him, bringing a paralytic who was carried by four men. And when they could not come near Him because of the crowd, they uncovered the roof where He was. So when they had broken through, they let down the bed on which the paralytic was lying."

Four men arrived too late to be able to get inside the house. But they had carried their paralytic friend on a bed, and they needed to get him to Jesus. When the four men got there, they may have said, "Ugh! How are we going to get our friend to Jesus? We can't even get through the door."

So these four men decided to take their friend, bed and all, up on the roof. That's pretty amazing! Now, dwellings in those days had stairs that went to the roof and a little place in the roof that could be opened. But that opening would not have been big enough to lower a full-grown man through it. Desperate to help their friend, these men tore into the structure of the roof to enable them to lower that man down to Jesus. That's persistence!

'Jesus Saw Their Faith'

Just imagine the scene: Jesus was simply preaching the Word to the crowd that had gathered. People were being encouraged and strengthened. They were seeing how amazing He was, and how He spoke with such authority. They were listening closely to every word.

Suddenly, there was quite a commotion over their heads. People watched as a paralyzed man on a mat was lowered from the rooftop into the room. As people looked up, they saw the faces of the four men looking down as the men gently placed their friend in front of Jesus.

Mark 2:5 says, "When Jesus saw their faith, He said to the paralytic, 'Son, your sins are forgiven you.'" Notice Jesus didn't say, "What's going on? Don't your friends have any manners? They've torn a hole in somebody's roof! What are they doing?" No, Jesus wasn't annoyed; He wasn't bothered. Jesus saw faith in the eyes and the actions of the persistent friends.

Jesus was teaching, and the faith of these men interrupted Jesus. And He said to the paralytic, "Son, your sins are forgiven you."

'That You May Know'

Jesus knew in His spirit that the scribes who were sitting in the room were reasoning in their hearts that nobody could forgive sins except for God alone. They were thinking, *Who is this guy? He blasphemes!* In His Spirit, Jesus knew exactly what they were thinking. Mark 2:8-11 says,

> **But immediately, when Jesus perceived in His spirit that they reasoned thus within themselves, He said to them, "Why do you reason about these things in your hearts? Which is easier, to say to the paralytic, 'Your sins are forgiven you,' or to say, 'Arise, take up your bed and walk'? But that you may know that the Son of Man has power on earth to forgive sins"** — He said

to the paralytic, "I say to you, arise, take up your bed, and go to your house."

In verse 10, the heart of Jesus is revealed: "But that you may know...." God wants us to *know*, beyond a shadow of a doubt, that not only does He forgive sins, but He heals — He is THE Healer. And Jesus Himself said, "Which is easier, to say to the paralytic, 'Your sins are forgiven you,' or to say, 'Arise, take up your bed and walk'?" We might say it this way: "Is there any difference in the power it takes to raise him from that bed than the power to forgive him of those sins?"

The story of the paralytic man and his faith-filled friends concludes in Mark 2:12, which says, "Immediately he [the paralytic man] arose, took up the bed, and went out in the presence of them all, so that all were amazed and glorified God, saying, 'We never saw anything like this!'"

Jesus Healed Them All

Just as Jesus paid the price for the sins of *all*, He paid the price for the sickness of *all*. In the Bible, it says 14 times that Jesus healed them *all*. Let's look at a few of these verses so faith can arise within us as we meditate on God's Word.

- "When evening had come, they brought to Him many who were demon-possessed. And He cast out the spirits with a word, and healed all who were sick" (Matthew 8:16).

- "And when Jesus went out He saw a great multitude; and He was moved with compassion for them, and healed their sick" (Matthew 14:14).

- "And great multitudes followed Him, and He healed them there" (Matthew 19:2).

- "Then the blind and the lame came to Him in the temple, and He healed them" (Matthew 21:14).

- "But when Jesus knew it, He withdrew from there. And great multitudes followed Him, and He healed them all" (Matthew 12:15).

And there are nine additional verses that, in various ways, say *Jesus healed them all*. We see so clearly that Jesus absolutely healed *all*. As Psalm 103:3 says, "Who forgives all your iniquities, Who heals all your diseases." He forgave *all* our iniquities, and He healed *all* our diseases. It's so important that this truth becomes *our* truth — and not just scriptures we skim past.

When someone is sick for a long time, this person may start to think, *Maybe God wants me to suffer. Maybe I am a testimony to others. Maybe this sickness is giving glory to God. Maybe God is trying to teach me something.* It's easy to start thinking those thoughts when the symptoms of an illness are screaming so loudly.

You may be struggling in your body and in the midst of a fight of faith. Doubts come, pain comes, and the doctor's report comes — it's a real fight! But imagine what will happen when you get your mind renewed to the truth in the Word of God that He is both your Savior *and* your Healer! It will increase and grow your faith so you can take hold of the truth and receive your healing.

Finis Dake, a biblical scholar, wrote the following commentary about Mark 2:12:

> God gets glory only in healing, not in the sickness. He may get glory out of some lives in spite of the sickness, but not because of it. Sickness should never be used as an excuse of glorifying God. One can glorify Him much better well than sick. He could testify to the same doctors and nurses while well as when sick if he would do so. He might argue that he never would have contacted them otherwise, but it is just as sensible to argue that he would miss others by being sick. We must be intelligent about biblical doctrines. If sickness is of Satan, as is clear in Matthew 8:17; Luke 13:16; John 10:10; Acts 10:38; etc., then it is not of God.

The truth that sickness is of Satan, not God, is made clear in Matthew, Mark, Luke, John, and Acts! Acts 10:38 says, "How God anointed Jesus of Nazareth with the Holy Spirit and with power, who went about doing good and healing all who were oppressed by the devil, for God was with Him." God anointed Jesus of Nazareth with the Holy Spirit and power. Sickness is of Satan — not of God!

In his commentary on Mark 2:12, Dake goes on to say,

> If sickness is of Satan, as is clear in Matthew 8:17; Luke 13:16; John 10:10; Acts 10:38; etc., then it is not of God. If such be of God, then He sent Jesus to destroy His own works. Then believers today are under command to destroy the works of God (Matthew 28:20; Mark 16:17,18; John 14:12). If sickness is of Satan, then healing must be of God, if done in the name of Jesus

Christ. As in this case and all others, if God became glorified by healing, then He was not glorified by the sickness. As long as the person was sick God did not get glory. Satan's work continued to be manifest and he was glorified up to the point of healing. To conclude otherwise would mean giving in to fallacy and unbelief, manifesting co-operation with Satan. When we quit accusing God of doing the work of Satan, recognize the true source of our trouble and then turn to God as the true source of help we shall begin to receive benefits.

What are those benefits? We find them in Psalm 103:2 and 3, which says, "Bless the Lord, O my soul, and forget not all His benefits: Who forgives all your iniquities, Who heals all your diseases." When Jesus died on the Cross, He took the beating, He took the slashing of His body, and He hung there. Jesus is not only your Savior, but He is absolutely your Healer as well.

Sickness does not give glory to God. But when we receive healing — oh, how it gives glory to God! You may have received healing before and shared your testimony and gave glory to God. Isn't the Word of God wonderful? The Bible clearly shows us that Jesus is not only our Savior — He's also 100 percent our Healer. And we have scripture to back it up.

The Lord absolutely forgives *all* your iniquities and heals *all* your diseases!

STUDY QUESTIONS

Be diligent to present yourself approved to God, a worker who does not need to be ashamed, rightly dividing the word of truth.
— 2 Timothy 2:15

1. Faith is action — it acts. It's *visible*. "They came to Him, bringing a paralytic who was carried by four men" (Mark 2:3). Due to the crowd, they climbed up to the roof, broke through the roof, and lowered their friend in front of the Healer. And "Jesus saw their faith" (Mark 2:5). The four men knew the paralytic would be healed if they could just get him to Jesus — and so they did! Faith that is alive, *acts*. Based on the following scriptures, how can you *act* in faith? (*Consider* James 2:18,20,26.)

2. Read Romans 10:17 and Romans 12:2. What do these scriptures tell you will happen as you read and hear God's Word?

You may be thinking, *I want to believe this with all my heart, but I need help.* Denise taught these lessons and wrote the book *Jesus Is Your Healer*, so the truth of God's healing Word can get even deeper inside you. Whatever it takes; get this teaching into your heart until you believe it. It will change your life!

PRACTICAL APPLICATION

**But be doers of the word,
and not hearers only, deceiving yourselves.**
— James 1:22

1. Psalm 103:3 says, "Who forgives all your iniquities, Who heals all your diseases." It's so important that this truth becomes *your* truth — and not just a scripture that you can recite. Take time to meditate on Psalm 103:3. Think about the word "all" — mentioned twice in this verse. "All" means that *no* sins and *no* diseases were left out when Jesus paid for them in your place.

2. When Jesus died on the Cross, He took the beating, He took the slashing of His body, and He hung there. Jesus is not only your Savior, but He is absolutely your Healer as well. If you've never received Jesus as your Healer, pray this prayer from your heart: *Lord, Jesus, I see from Your Word that You not only took my sins, but You also paid for my healing. I receive You as my Healer right now. In Jesus' name. Amen.*

3. This lesson displays the persistent faith of a good friend. What kind of friend are you to others? Is there someone you know who needs healing? Take a moment to get in touch with them now and share the powerful truths you have learned from these lessons.

---

[1] Finis Jennings Dake, *Dake's Annotated Reference Bible: The Holy Bible* (Lawrenceville, GA: Dake Bible Sales, Inc., 1963), 36.

[2] Ibid.

TOPIC

Hope Opens the Door for Healing

SCRIPTURES

1. **1 Corinthians 13:13** — And now abide faith, hope, love, these three; but the greatest of these is love.

2. **Mark 5:25-34** — Now a certain woman had a flow of blood for twelve years, and had suffered many things from many physicians. She had spent all that she had and was no better, but rather grew worse. When she heard about Jesus, she came behind Him in the crowd and touched His garment. For she said, "If only I may touch His clothes, I shall be made well." Immediately the fountain of her blood was dried up, and she felt in her body that she was healed of the affliction. And Jesus, immediately knowing in Himself that power had gone out of Him, turned around in the crowd and said, "Who touched My clothes?" But His disciples said to Him, "You see the multitude thronging You, and You say, 'Who touched Me?'" And He looked around to see her who had done this thing. But the woman, fearing and trembling, knowing what had happened to her, came and fell down before Him and told Him the whole truth. And He said to her, "Daughter, your faith has made you well. Go in peace, and be healed of your affliction."

3. **Hebrews 11:6** — But without faith it is impossible to please Him, for he who comes to God must believe that He is, and that He is a rewarder of those who diligently seek Him.

4. **1 John 5:4** — ...And this is the victory that has overcome the world — our faith.

SYNOPSIS

In Mark 5:25-34, we learn about the woman who suffered for 12 years with an issue of blood. Her sickness made her unclean in the eyes of other people, and she had spent all her money on doctors and medicines, but nothing helped. But when she heard about Jesus, faith arose within her, which gave her the courage to pursue Jesus and receive her healing.

The emphasis of this lesson:

Pain and sickness have a loud voice. But God's Word is louder and stronger, and it silences the voice of the enemy. When we find ourselves in a fight of faith against sickness, hearing and speaking the Word of God gives us faith to overcome.

'I Met Up With Hope'

On the program, Denise shared her testimony to encourage you. God is no respecter of persons (*see* Acts 10:34) — He shows no partiality. His healing power is for all people, including you! May hope arise in you now as you read this because what He does for others, He'll do for you!

> Many years ago, when I was about 25 years old, I'd had a disease for 13 years. I didn't know that Jesus was my Healer. I knew Him as my Savior, but I didn't know Him as my Healer yet.
>
> One day I heard a man on the radio declare Isaiah 53:5: "By His stripes, you are healed," and that's when I met up with hope. I don't mean, "I *hope* I am healed." No, this is more powerful than that. This is a hope that has expectancy. When I heard that scripture from that radio preacher, hope came alive in me!
>
> You know, when you have a disease for 13 years, you begin to think that this is going to be your life. I had no hope of it ever changing. But when I heard that preacher declare that I had been healed by the stripes that Jesus took on His body, that's when hope came into my heart — and it changed everything! And I said to the Lord, "You mean I can be healed?"
>
> A few months later, I went to bed with the disease I had had on my face for 13 years — it was still there. But when I woke up the next morning, I was completely healed.

Hope Is Powerful!

First Corinthians 13:13 says, "And now abide faith, hope, love, these three; but the greatest of these is love." Notice that *hope* is in there. Let's look at a woman in the Bible who was facing a hopeless situation, but hope came into her heart and changed everything. Mark 5:25-34 says,

Now a certain woman had a flow of blood for twelve years, and had suffered many things from many physicians. She had spent all that she had and was no better, but rather grew worse. When she heard about Jesus, she came behind Him in the crowd and touched His garment. For she said, "If only I may touch His clothes, I shall be made well."

Immediately the fountain of her blood was dried up, and she felt in her body that she was healed of the affliction. And Jesus, immediately knowing in Himself that power had gone out of Him, turned around in the crowd and said, "Who touched My clothes?"

But His disciples said to Him, "You see the multitude thronging You, and You say, 'Who touched Me?'"

And He looked around to see her who had done this thing. But the woman, fearing and trembling, knowing what had happened to her, came and fell down before Him and told Him the whole truth. And He said to her, "Daughter, your faith has made you well. Go in peace, and be healed of your affliction."

Oh, what a powerful story! This was a woman who had spent all her money over the years in search of a cure for her disease but to no avail. But then she heard about Jesus — and we can imagine what she heard. Maybe she heard about the blind eyes that had been opened (*see* Mark 10:46-52). Maybe she heard about the little boy who had been delivered from demons (*see* Mark 9:14-29). Or maybe she heard about the thousands of hungry people whom Jesus had fed, spiritually and physically (*see* Matthew 14:13-21).

We're not sure what this woman heard, but the Bible clearly says *she heard* (v. 27). And what happened when she heard? Hope came into her heart — just like the hope that entered Denise's heart when she heard the radio preacher declare, "By His stripes, you are healed.!"

Faith for Healing Rose Up

The woman with the issue of blood had been on a very challenging journey. For 12 years she had suffered from a constant flow of blood from her body, so the religious law of that day would have deemed her "unclean." And as an unclean woman, she would have been prohibited from interacting with normal society to avoid "contaminating" anyone else. If she sat on something, and then somebody else sat on it, that person would also be considered unclean. If she touched somebody, that person would also be deemed unclean — all because of her constant flow of blood. The isolation and depth of rejection this woman carried in her soul must have been almost unbearable.

You may or may not have ever had a sickness like this woman's issue of blood, but perhaps you can imagine what she was thinking as hope started to arise in her heart: *Maybe I CAN be healed. Maybe I can be rid of this horrible disease that I've carried in my body for 12 years. I've wasted so much money on doctors, and they didn't help me. But maybe Jesus can help me.*

It certainly doesn't make sense in the natural that she would think simply touching His clothes would bring healing to her body, but she must have had thoughts similar to these: *If I can just touch Jesus' clothes! I don't have to look at Him. I don't have to touch His skin. He doesn't have to touch me. But if I could just — for a split-second — touch His clothes, I know that I would be healed.* It's just amazing that she would think this, but that's what was in her heart. She believed if she could just touch Him, she would be healed.

She Focused on Reaching Jesus

When the woman with the issue of blood heard the testimonies about Jesus, she started making her way to Him. Just imagine what it would have been like for this woman: She left her house, and the door closed behind her. She was now out in the open — blood still flowing from her body.

She was probably exhausted and scared. We can imagine her thoughts: *What if somebody sees me, and they yell, "Unclean" at me? Then what am I going to do? Oh, I don't care! I just know that if I touch His clothes, I'm going to be healed. I've got to do this.* Then she saw the crowd and she said to herself, *Well, here I go.* And she got on the ground, crawling her way through the crowd, and making her way through all the feet. Scholars say that she probably got on the ground because she wanted to remain unnoticed.

And then she saw Jesus' garment! She may have heard His voice or the voices of other people telling Him their problems. She may have heard the voice of Jairus, a very powerful man and a leader in the synagogue, who came to Jesus to ask Him to heal his daughter.

But she saw the garment of Jesus, and said to herself, *This is my chance.* She reached out and touched the hem of Jesus' garment. And Mark 5:29

says, "Immediately the fountain of her blood was dried up, and she felt in her body that she was healed of the affliction."

The Power of Just One Touch

Have you ever had to endure something for five years? Ten years? It was twelve long years that this disease had taken this woman's energy. It had taken her time and her money. But when she touched Jesus' garment, suddenly — in an instant — the unhealthy flow of her blood completely stopped.

But what happened after that? Jesus said, in effect, "Who touched Me? Somebody touched Me. I felt it. Who touched Me? Who is it?" And He began turning around, looking all around the crowd to find who had touched Him (*see* v. 30). The woman must have thought, *Oh no! The secret I've been trying to keep is out. I'm unclean. I'm not unclean now, but I touched Him. The secret is out.*

Her story continues, "And He looked around to see her who had done this thing. But the woman, fearing and trembling, knowing what had happened to her, came and fell down before Him and told Him the whole truth" (Mark 5:32,33).

We don't know exactly what this woman told Jesus, but we can imagine she shared her story. Maybe she said, "I'm healed, Jesus! I've been bleeding for 12 years, and it's been so horrible. I've gone to so many doctors, and I've spent so much money, all my money, and I have no more. But I wasn't getting any better. But then, Jesus, *I heard about You!* I heard that You healed a little boy that had demons, and he was free after You touched him and prayed for him. I heard that blind eyes were opened. And I just thought, if You could do that for them, then You could do that for me — I just needed to get to You." She may have told him everything.

God's Heart of Compassion Is for All of Us

The Bible says that Jesus responded to this woman's story so tenderly. He didn't say, "Woman, thank you for your story, but here stands Jairus. Do you know who he is? He is a leader in the synagogue and his daughter is really, really sick. I've got to go and help Jairus because he's powerful. I'm glad you're healed. Thank you for your story, but I need to go."

No, Jesus didn't do that. He took the time to talk to Jairus, and He took the time to talk to this woman, who was an outcast of society. He said to her, "Daughter, your faith has made you well. Go in peace, and be healed of your affliction" (Mark 5:34).

What a wonderful Savior! What a wonderful Healer! And Hebrews 1:3 says that Jesus is the express image of God the Father. When we read about Jesus in the Bible, we see that He took the time to let somebody who was an outcast of society tell her story. He wasn't trying to make her hurry. He wasn't putting her down because she wasn't as powerful as Jairus, a leader of the synagogue. No, Jesus saw her. That's the heart of Jesus! And that's the heart of the Father. Whatever station in life you are in — whatever you've done or haven't done — He is the same right now as He was then. You are important to Him, and He sees you.

Hebrews 13:8 says, "Jesus Christ is the same yesterday, today, and forever." So the Father's heart of compassion is the same to you today as it was to the woman with the issue of blood then. Do you think that someone powerful, with more money and more prestige, is more important to Jesus than you? No! In fact, we see in the gospels that Jesus would come to those who were the most rejected by society. He's no respecter of persons — He does not show favoritism (*see* Acts 10:34).

Receive Your Healing by Faith

Just picture for a moment what was happening in the events outlined in Mark 5:25-34. All those people were crowded around Jesus. And there stood Jairus, who was worried about his daughter — she was about to die. Because of his position in the synagogue, Jairus could walk right up to Jesus and get His attention.

But how did the woman with the issue of blood get Jesus' attention? It wasn't that she was standing in front of Jesus that caught His attention. It was her *faith* that drew His attention to her. Hebrews 11:6 says, "But without faith it is impossible to please Him, for he who comes to God must believe that He is, and that He is a rewarder of those who diligently seek Him." And First John 5:4 declares, "…And this is the victory that has overcome the world — our faith." We overcome in this world by our faith.

This is Truth! Jesus is your Savior, and He is your Healer. Yes, He has given you a new nature on the inside. In Him, you are the righteousness of God. You have the Holy Spirit inside you — you have the love of God inside you. If you have received Jesus as your Lord and Savior, this is all true about you. But Jesus also paid for your healing. Every sickness and disease was nailed to the Cross, and "By His stripes, *you are healed*" (*see* Isaiah 53:5). He paid the complete price — and now, it's for you to receive by faith.

When the woman with the issue of blood heard about Jesus, hope came into her heart, and she said to herself, *If I can just touch the hem of His garment, I will be healed.* Faith was operating inside her — all the way through the crowd to the feet of Jesus. And she was completely healed!

Do you need a touch from Jesus? Just one touch of His power can eradicate every sickness, disease, and pain in your body. He is your magnificent Savior and Healer. And it's His absolute will to not only save you but to heal you!

STUDY QUESTIONS

Be diligent to present yourself approved to God, a worker who does not need to be ashamed, rightly dividing the word of truth.
— 2 Timothy 2:15

1. When Denise heard the radio preacher say, "By His stripes, you were healed" (*see* Isaiah 53:5 and 1 Peter 2:24), hope came into her heart. Hebrews 11:1 says that faith is "the substance of things hoped for, the evidence of things not seen." What else does the Bible say about the power of hope? (*Consider* Romans 15:13 and Hebrews 6:19.)

2. Jesus said to the woman with the issue of blood, "Daughter, your faith has made you well" (Mark 5:34). What other Bible examples show us that the individual's faith made them well? (*Consider* Matthew 9:28,29; Luke 18:41-43; and Acts 14:9,10.)

3. The woman with the issue of blood was healed when she touched Jesus' garment. Meditate on the steps that led to her healing. Mark 5:27 and 28 says, "When she *heard* about Jesus, she *came* behind Him in the crowd and *touched* His garment. For she *said,* 'If only I may touch His clothes, I shall be made well.'"
    *   **"She heard."** Faith rose in her heart when she heard the truth — that Jesus heals. "Faith comes by hearing, and hearing by the word of God" (*see* Romans 10:17).

- **"She came."** She acted in faith by coming to Jesus and touching His garment. "Faith without works is dead" (*see* James 2:20).

- **"She said."** She received exactly what she said: "If only I may touch His clothes, I shall be made well." Mark 11:23 says, "For assuredly, I say to you, whoever says to this mountain, 'Be removed and be cast into the sea,' and does not doubt in his heart, but believes that those things he says will be done, he will have whatever he says."

PRACTICAL APPLICATION

**But be doers of the word,
and not hearers only, deceiving yourselves.**
—James 1:22

1. As Denise mentioned, "The isolation and depth of rejection this woman [with the issue of blood] carried in her soul must have been almost unbearable." If you've struggled with feelings of rejection, come to Jesus and pour out your heart before Him. Know that God accepts you! Then, just like sitting at the edge of the ocean and allowing cool water to wash over you as wave after wave comes in, allow the truth in the following scriptures to wash over you and "restore your soul" (Psalm 23:3).

   - "He made us accepted in the Beloved" (*see* Ephesians 1:6).

   - "When my father and my mother forsake me, then the Lord will take me up" (Psalm 27:10).

   - "See what [an incredible] quality of love the Father has given (shown, bestowed on) us, that we should [be permitted to] be named and called and counted the children of God! And so we are!" (*see* 1 John 3:1 *AMPC*).

2. Embrace the power of His sacrifice both to save and to heal you! When the woman with the issue of blood heard about Jesus, faith came into her heart. Her faith made *her* whole, and your faith can make *you* whole! Take time to meditate on the scriptures in these lessons. Allow them to renew your mind to the truth: Jesus paid for both your sins *and* sicknesses. Write down the scriptures that resonate in your heart and share these vital truths with a friend or family member in need of healing!

CLAIM YOUR FREE RESOURCE!

As a way of introducing you further to the teaching ministry of Rick Renner, we would like to send you FREE of charge his teaching, "How To Receive a Miraculous Touch From God" on CD or as an MP3 download.

In His earthly ministry, Jesus commonly healed *all* who were sick of *all* their diseases. In this profound message, learn about the manifold dimensions of Christ's wisdom, goodness, power, and love toward all humanity who came to Him in faith with their needs.

☑ **YES, I want to receive Rick Renner's monthly teaching letter!**

Simply scan the QR code to claim this resource or go to: **renner.org/claim-your-free-offer**

Connect

WITH US!

www.ingramcontent.com/pod-product-compliance
Lightning Source LLC
Chambersburg PA
CBHW071650040426
42452CB00009B/1824